Shall We

by
Anne Barton
Parish Deacon of St. John the Baptist, Burley, Hampshire

GROVE BOOKS LIMITED
Bramcote   Nottingham   NG9 3DS

CONTENTS

THE COVER PICTURE

is by Peter Ashton

First Impression October 1991

ISSN 0144-171X
ISBN 1 85174 193 3

FOREWORD

by the Bishop of Southampton, The Rt. Rev. John F. Perry
The purpose of this booklet 'to examine the use of dance and movement from the perspective of the worship leader' is admirably fulfilled by its author. Anne Barton has researched and given practical application to her material with meticulous care and imagination. She takes us on a fascinating journey through the relevant Biblical and historical sources, continually holding the reader's interest. Negative reactions to dance in worship are faced and handled with a firm sensitivity. She looks carefully at the need to redress the balance in the attitude of the church to human sexuality, and how this inevitably affects some reactions to dance in worship. We are rightly reminded that dance in worship must have the supreme aim to glorify God.

The practical chapters on the development and introduction of dance in worship bring the possibility of dance within the reach of any and every congregation. The final chapter on 'The Dance Group' spells out the basis on which a leader needs to be appointed and a group formed, with the group's own spiritual life being the centre from which any creative dance will emerge. 'The dance of the group will grow out of the worshipping life of the group.'

This is a gem of a booklet and I commend it most warmly. I hope that we will receive more from the pen of its author!

1. INTRODUCTION

What is liturgical dance? Is it 'Ring-a-ring-o'-roses around the altar'? Is it a grand name used to persuade entire congregations to participate in the 'action songs' formerly thought to come in the province of the children's work? Is it some of the young (or not so young) women of the congregation cavorting in leotards? This is an area where preconceived ideas and misconceptions abound; many such remarks have been the response to the preparation of this booklet. Two reactions have been the most common. One has been that described elsewhere by Gordon and Ronni Lamont of Kinetik Theatre:

'Someone was talking to us about what we do. The word "dance" sparked off the reaction.

' "Oh gee", she said (she was American), "I saw some dance once in church. A group of girls dressed up in beautiful flowing robes and they waved their arms about like this ..." ("this" was a sort of wafting-tree-branches-in-the-breeze type movement) "... and they smiled..." (this bit would have made an excellent toothpaste ad) "... and I thought it was just great you know. I guess that's what you do isn't it?" '[1]

The other common response has been from those who have genuine misgivings about whether dance should be allowed at all. As with church music, we all approach liturgical dance with our own ideas of what is or is not appropriate in worship; but whereas the overwhelming majority of Christians would agree on the principle of using music in worship, there are many who would question the use of dance. So, in discussing liturgical dance, it is necessary to have a clear definition of what the term includes.

Dance is here being interpreted in the general sense of movement that is, or could be, choreographed. This definition includes all the possibilities envisaged above but also moves wider to include all the movement that is a necessary part of shared worship. In an earlier book in this series Trevor Lloyd has made the case that ceremonial in worship is inevitable; it is 'formal, repeatable, religious action', and will develop in any group that worships together.[2] The movement may vary from the most elaborate of processions to a simple change of posture but in every case is a physical expression of worship that has become a ritual movement whose meaning can, we hope, be understood. Even in churches that aim for a deliberate absence of ceremonial or movement, that in itself becomes its own ritual and in doing so makes a statement about what that congregation believes worship to be.

The question of what movement is allowed, encouraged, or forbidden in worship touches on fundamental questions about the Christian understanding of humanity, and about the true expression of that humanity in relationship to God in worship. Such issues lie behind the doubts and uncertainties that emerge when the introduction of dance is proposed. While there is now a growing enthusiasm for dance in worship, this has

[1] G. and R. Lamont, *Move Yourselves* (Bible Society, 1983), p.25.
[2] Trevor Lloyd, *Ceremonial in Worship*, (Grove Worship Series No.75, 1981).

not been the case for most of the two thousand years of the Church. A review of the history of dance in the Church will show that while there has generally been dancing associated with the life of the Christian community, the official attitude has often been disapproval and prohibition. If we now wish to encourage dance in worship it would be irresponsible not to be aware of the factors that led to this attitude. Many of these factors will be seen to originate from doctrines of humanity that are not in accordance with the Biblical view, and their validity will therefore be questioned. However, this is not done merely to satisfy those who are seeking a justification for dance in worship, but with the wider perspective of working towards a more truly Christian understanding of human nature, which can inform and enrich every aspect of our worship.

Because the questions raised by the use of dance in worship are so fundamental, it is essential that they are handled at a theological and historical level as well as a purely practical one. That is not to dismiss the practical skills. However, much of the literature currently available on dance in worship concentrates on the practical know-how required by dance leaders, without addressing the theological and historical issues in any depth. Such practical material is extremely valuable to those engaged in a dance ministry and its importance is not to be under-estimated. The use of any art form in worship is not entirely independent of its use in other contexts; the choirmaster training the choir is using the same skills as he does when giving singing lessons. In worship, however, the primary focus is not on the artistic skills in themselves but on their use as a vehicle for the expression of worship. That is why it is not sufficient to be content with the practical skills.

The purpose of this booklet is to examine the use of dance and movement in worship from the perspective of the worship leader. Whether that person is an expert dancer or not is immaterial. Their concern as worship leader is for the means by which the people of God are enabled to offer their worship. The use of dance has to come within that primary purpose, and should not be hived off into a specialist corner 'for those who like that sort of thing'. Those who lead worship need to understand the part played by movement and dance in worship and should not abdicate their responsibility for the decisions about its use; those who wish to dance in worship need to understand the context of worship within which they dance.

The remaining chapters of this booklet therefore address the question of the use of dance in worship from historical, theological and practical perspectives. By being aware of the issues raised by the consideration of movement in worship, those concerned with the preparation and leading of shared worship will be asking important questions about worship. What does the way we worship say about the God to whom it is addressed? Does what we do enable others to offer their worship to God? Which aspects of our humanity are celebrated, which are brought to God for his healing, and which ignored? What has become the accepted liturgical practice of our church, and why? Are those reasons still valid, or are we just doing what we've always done because 'we've always done it that way'? These are the sort of questions that those responsible for worship need to be prepared to ask.

2. DID THEY DANCE?

The history of dance in worship

(a) The universality of religious dance

Modern Western culture is unusual in regarding dance as secular rather than sacred. It has been far more common for dance to be part of the ritual associated with religion, and the distinction between sacred and secular would not necessarily have been made; 'dance was bound up with life itself, and life was intimately bound up with religion.'[1] This is apparent from the records that survive of ancient cultures all over the world. It can also be seen in the current practice of religions that pre-date Christianity, for example in Hindu temple dancing and at Buddhist and Shinto shrines. While such practices in other religions in no way give authority to the use of dance in Christian worship, the universality of dance as a means of offering worship demands that serious consideration is given to the validity of the reasons why Christians have often rejected it.

(b) The Old Testament

There can be little doubt that the expression of worship in ancient Israel included dance. The Old Testament makes frequent mention of the festivals which were the focal points of the year. The word translated as 'festival' was the chief Hebrew word for 'dance'. It can therefore be assumed that dancing was an integral part of these celebrations. That would account for any lack of specific instructions about dance on such occasions. As A.A. Anderson points out in his commentary on Psalm 87: 'Dancing is not described in detail by the OT writers, but the activity must have been common enough not to require a special mention.'[2]

It is evident that these festivals included processions[3], instrumental music[4], singing[5], shouting[6] and clapping[7]; dancing would be entirely in keeping with the nature of such celebrations.

Specific references to dancing support this picture of the use of dance in worship in ancient Israel. There are the general injunctions of Psalm 149.3 and Psalm 150.4, that the people should 'praise his name with dancing', as well as with trumpet, lute, and harp, with strings and pipe and cymbals. There is Miriam dancing to celebrate the parting of the waters and Israel's rescue from the Egyptians.[8] There are the daughters of Shiloh dancing at the yearly feast[9]; whatever else may be questionable about this story, it is apparent that the dancing formed an accepted part of celebration.

[1] Martin Blogg, *Dance and the Christian Faith*, (Hodder and Stoughton, 1985), p.9.
[2] A.A. Anderson, *Psalms (73-150)*, New Century Bible Commentary, (Marshall, Morgan & Scott, 1972), p.622.
[3] Psalm 68.24-25.
[4] Psalm 98.5-6.
[5] Psalm 96.1.
[6] Psalm 89.15.
[7] Psalm 47.1.
[8] Exodus 15.20.
[9] Judges 21.19.

Where dancing appears to be criticized in the Old Testament, it is necessary to look at the context in order to see what is actually being censured, and by whom. In Exodus 32, there is the account of how the people of Israel make a golden calf and worship it and sacrifice to it, and there is dancing. When Moses returns from Sinai and sees 'the calf and the dancing'[1] he breaks the tablets of the law and the golden calf is ground to powder. It can be seen that the activity of dancing does not in itself warrant criticism. The dancing is the offering of worship; what is wrong is not that the worship is danced, but that it is not offered to God. Far from being a criticism of danced worship *per se*, this passage actually assumes dance to be a valid expression of worship, sufficiently common not to require comment.

The other well-known example of dancing in the Old Testament is David 'dancing with all his might' as the ark of the covenant is brought into the city.[2] This too is criticized; but in this case, the criticism comes from David's wife Michal. R.P. Gordon in his commentary[3] makes the point that her criticism, though ostensibly of the dancing, probably has much wider implications; in any case David is clear that his dancing is in honour of the Lord, and the conclusion of the chapter suggests that it is Michal who is in the wrong. So again, dance emerges as a means of expressing worship which is in itself acceptable.

Dancing is clearly linked with celebration, and as such is an expression of praise and thanksgiving. It conveys a sense of physical exuberance which cannot be contained. That sense of exuberance is also transmitted in the metaphorical use of dance language, which reflects and extends the experience of dance in worship. For example:
> 'the mountains skipped like rams
> the hills like lambs.'[4]

and:
> 'Let the sea roar, and all that fills it;
> the world and those who dwell in it!
> Let the floods clap their hands;
> let the hills sing for joy together
> before the Lord'.[5]

The use of such metaphor speaks strongly of a culture in which such elements of leaping and skipping, clapping and singing, were part of the people's experience of worship.

Further indication that dance was associated with celebration is given by the use of 'dancing' as the opposite of 'mourning', as in the series of contrasts given in Ecclesiastes 4: 'a time to mourn, and a time to dance'. This could be thought to mean that the use of movement in worship is to be restricted to praise and thanksgiving, to celebration. However, to do this would be to miss the range of physical expression that is given to other emotions in the Old Testament. The sackcloth and shaved heads of

---

[1] Exodus 32.19.
[2] 2 Samuel 6.14.
[3] R. P. Gordon, *1 & 2 Samuel*, (Paternoster, 1986), p.234.
[4] Psalm 114.4.
[5] Psalm 98.7-8.

mourning or repentance, the hands lifted in prayer, the knees bent in adoration, were all part of the expression of the relationship between the Israelites and their God. 'Dance' is now understood in Western cultures as a term with a wider meaning that would include movement expressing the whole range of human emotion. All of this would have had parallels in the worship of ancient Israel.

(c) The New Testament

Turning to the New Testament from the Old, the lack of references to dance in worship in the New Testament is immediately apparent, and this has led some Christians to question whether dance should find a place in Christian worship at all. Dance, they would argue, is scarcely mentioned in the New Testament; such references as there are, are not in the context of worship and do not support the principle of dance in worship. The conclusion is then drawn that if dance was part of Old Testament worship but is not mentioned in the New Testament, then this was a feature of Judaism that Christianity rejected.

Such an argument does not take into account the continuity of the Old and New Testaments. Jesus' life and ministry are set within the culture of Judaism. As Martin Blogg has commented:

'Jesus was a Jew and as such the Old Testament was his prayer book and teaching. Since he was a Jew it is as certain that he danced as it is that he wore a beard.'[1]

The way in which Jesus uses the illustration of the children playing at weddings[2] shows that dancing at weddings was a commonplace part of the celebration, and it is difficult to imagine that the Lord who provided wine at the wedding at Cana[3] could have disapproved of the dancing without there being some record of that.

The imagery of the parable of the Prodigal Son lends support to the idea that Jesus saw dancing as a natural part of celebration. On the return of the prodigal, the father gives instructions that they are all to 'eat and make merry', and the elder son returns from the fields to hear 'music and dancing'.[4] Remembering that this is in a culture in which the divisions of secular and sacred were not drawn in the way which is familiar to us, Jesus is here describing an occasion of celebration and thanksgiving. Given the implications of the parable, it can be seen that the celebration in music and dance instigated by the father in the parable parallels the rejoicing in heaven over the sinner who repents. Had Jesus been intending to introduce the opposition of the expression of rejoicing and celebration in dance in a culture where this was accepted, it seems unlikely that he would have drawn such parallels in his teaching.

But, just as in the Old Testament the dancing offered in worship to the golden calf serves as a reminder that dancing can be misused, in the Gospels there is the account of Salome dancing in the episode which leads to

[1] Martin Blogg, op. cit., p.5.
[2] Matthew 11.17.
[3] John 2.
[4] Luke 15.23-24.

the execution of John the Baptist.[1] Although the Biblical account is restrained, commentators are agreed that this dancing would have been a deliberately provocative performance, like the dancing of the solo dancers of Greece and Rome who were prostitutes and of poor moral reputation. Salome's dancing can in no way be described as honouring God; it is motivated by greed, revenge, and personal ambition, and achieves its ends by deliberate exploitation and abuse of human sexuality. This episode stands with the golden calf incident as a sobering reminder that dance can be misused, and, given the weakness of human nature, is likely to be misused. But so are all of God's gifts to us. We do not prohibit food because some over-indulge. For dance, as for all God's gifts, the appropriate response to abuse is not neglect or prohibition, but proper use.

(d) The early church
In his book *Liturgical Dance*[2] J. G. Davies gives a detailed account of the church's attitude to dance throughout its history. He emphasizes that it is important to consider the evidence from any period *in the context of its time*. This takes into account the way in which Christians were responding to the culture in which they found themselves: the extent to which they were able to assimilate the values of their society and incorporate them into Christian practice without compromising their faith, and the extent to which Christians felt the need to be distinctively different from those around them.

Davies maintains that this awareness of the prevailing cultural milieu is of particular significance in assessing the condemnation of dance that developed during the Patristic period. This is partly because the bounds of Christian orthodoxy were laid down at that time, and because of that the writings of that period have since commanded a particular authority. It is also because of the influence of the Fathers on those who were responsible for the doctrines of the Reformation in the sixteenth century, and hence on the doctrine and practice of their churches ever since. These are comments that apply to the assessment of the Patristic evidence on any issue; the question of the use of dance in worship raises the particular difficulty of how something indigenous to Jewish worship, which Jesus himself did not single out for criticism but seems rather to have accepted, and which is neither rejected nor re-interpreted for Christians in the New Testament, could have become the subject of such fierce condemnation.

This is why it is important to assess the documentary evidence against its setting in the culture of the Roman Empire. As Christianity spread around the Mediterranean world, the background of the adherents of the new faith was conditioned by the Greek and Roman world, rather than by the history and traditions of Israel. Dancing played its part in the worship of the pagan cults, and had at this time become debased to the point where it was a degrading display of eroticism, a view that was held by the authors of pagan writings as well as Christian. In a culture where 'dance' had such implications, the suggestion that Christian worship should include dance could have been seriously misunderstood by those who were uncertain as

[1] Mark 6.17-29.
[2] J. G. Davies, *Liturgical Dance*, (SCM, 1984).

to what was expected of them. The shared meal of the eucharist seems to have posed problems enough in Corinth . . .[1]

As well as needing to be distinct from the pagan culture around them, Christianity needed to become distinct from Judaism, as the divisions between church and synagogue hardened into separation. Part of this process was the way in which steps were taken to ensure that Christian and Jewish worship could not be confused. The Didache includes the following instruction:
'Do not keep the same fast-days as the hypocrites [*i.e.* the Jews]. Mondays and Thursdays are their days for fasting, so yours should be Wednesdays and Fridays.'[2]
Disapproval of dance would have had the effect of distancing Christian worship from the worship of others who used dance; pagans, Jews, and some of the heretical Christian sects as is apparent from writings such as the *Acts of John* and the *Acts of Thomas*.

Whatever other factors may have influenced Christian attitudes to dance, the one that has undoubtedly had the most far-reaching effects has been the predominance of Greek philosophical thought. Of particular significance is the Platonic dualism that separates soul and body. The extreme form of dualism was propounded in Manichaeism, which held that matter was evil and the human body as part of the material order was evil. Christian theologians did not generally go as far as that, following rather those whose philosophy recognized the material world as essentially good rather than evil, but of less significance and reality than the spiritual realm. What emerged from this was the interpretation of the New Testament in terms of the prevailing Greek philosophy, resulting in the views that have dominated Christian teaching ever since; of the soul and body as separate, the 'I' of personality being identified with the soul which was seen as immortal rather than with the body which was not.

Against such a background the Christian Church tended towards asceticism and monasticism as its ideals. Dance, already being denigrated as a debased art by the culture of the time, was not going to win approval from the Church which placed the emphasis so much on the spiritual rather than the material:
'The tide of adverse opinion was in full flow and was not to be stemmed throughout the next millennium; indeed a whole series of councils (albeit none ecumenical and most of restricted local reference) proceeded to place dancing under a ban.'[3]

Two points emerge from the Patristic evidence. Firstly, the Fathers could and did assign a spiritual meaning to dance, following Plato and others who had used this imagery. Dance is used metaphorically by Christian authors to portray not only the life of heaven, but also the Christian pattern of life, without necessarily implying literal dance at all. Secondly, dancing undoubtedly did continue among Christians. The very fact that repeated injunctions against dancing were required is itself evidence that dancing was not so easily to be abandoned.

[1] 1 Corinthians 1.17ff.
[2] *The Didache*, in M. Staniforth (ed.), *Early Christian Writings*, (Penguin, 1987), p.194.
[3] J. G. Davies, *op. cit.*, p.28.

During the centuries of Christendom, the pressure to be a distinctive minority gradually disappeared, and by mediaeval times there is ample evidence for dancing in churches. The church had become the focus of the community and the church building would often have been the only large building. The feast days of the church were the holidays (holy days) and so the celebrations of community life were intimately bound up with the festivals of the church. Many festival processions and carols now regarded as traditional originate from this period and provide an indication of the dancing that was taking place.

(e) The Reformation and beyond
A negative attitude to dance does begin to assert itself again at the time of the Reformation, but it is not as uniformly and totally negative as is sometimes thought. Luther accepted dancing at weddings; as with music, the Lutheran churches allowed much that the Calvinists rejected. The disappearance of dance from the churches that begins in the sixteenth century Reformation can, in its early stages, be attributed as much to neglect as to condemnation. Much of the initiative of the Reformation was dependent on the newly invented printing press, which made possible the rapid dissemination of the ideals of the Christian humanists, notably Erasmus. His satirical works focused the attention of Europe on the corruption of the mediaeval Church, and his publication of the Greek New Testament was the foundation on which the vernacular translations of the Bible were laid. There was a new enthusiasm for the reading and exposition of Scripture, typified by the Preface to the Book of Common Prayer of 1549:

> '. . . the whole Bible (or the greatest part thereof) should be read over once every year; intending thereby, that the Clergy, and especially such as were Ministers in the congregation, should (by often reading, and meditation in God's word) be stirred up to godliness themselves, and be more able to exhort others by wholesome doctrine, and to confute them that were adversaries to the truth; and further, that the people (by daily hearing of holy Scripture read in the Church) might continually profit more and more in the knowledge of God, and be the more inflamed with the love of his true religion.'

This emphasis on Scripture constituted a drastic swing of the pendulum away from the attitudes and practices of the mediaeval Church to a cerebral and literate approach to worship. With attention focused on the translation of Scripture and liturgies into the vernacular, a high value was placed on reading, hearing and understanding, an attitude succinctly described by the Collect for the Second Sunday in Advent. The contribution of visual and physical expression in worship was played down, particularly where the Reformers saw that this had allowed the incorporation of 'many things, whereof some are untrue, some uncertain, some vain and superstitious'.[1] It is no coincidence that it is from this period onwards that church furnishing is dominated by pew and pulpit, as worship became dominated by the spoken word. This meant that the open naves of the mediaeval churches were filled with furniture and any possibility of dancing in church has, until recent architectural innovations in church design, been restricted as much by that as by any other consideration.

The nostalgia of the Renaissance that looked back to ancient Greece and Rome as a golden age played its part in the thinking of the Christian humanists, contributing to the desire to recapture the doctrines of the early Church, stripped of the layers of mediaeval accretions. The respect in which they held the Fathers was second only to the authority of Scripture itself. Where dancing is condemned by the Reformers, it is sometimes a reflection of their enthusiasm for the rediscovered writings of the Fathers, and the injunctions against dance to be found in the Fathers are repeated. This is particularly true of Calvin, who banned dancing in Geneva in 1547.

The well-known Puritan dislike of dancing became established in the seventeenth century, rather than the sixteenth. It was characteristic of the widening gulf between the Church of England and the Puritans, that the Church of England was prepared to accept that which was not expressly forbidden in Scripture while the Puritans rejected that which was not expressly commanded. Echoes of these two ways of applying Scripture still surface today in debates over the use of dance in worship . . .

The developments of the eighteenth and nineteenth centuries reflect the prevailing philosophy of their time, and are reminiscent of the early centuries of the Church. Just as the Church was then profoundly influenced by neo-Platonic philosophy, so the Church in the eighteenth and nineteenth centuries showed the influence of the Enlightenment. The dualism that separated body and soul had long been an accepted part of Christian thinking, and the philosophy of Descartes continued in the same vein and reinforced this compartmental approach to human nature by emphasising the mind as opposed to the body. In an age dominated by reason, the aspects of life that were not amenable to logic and proof became neglected, as the pursuit of scientific knowledge and developing industrialisation took centre stage in Western culture. By the Victorian era, dance was regarded as a frivolous pastime; it was certainly not considered to have any place in worship. The Western separation of life into the sacred and the secular had followed from the compartmentalizing of human experience, and dance had acquired the label 'secular'.

(f) Recent developments

Dancing continued into the 20th century as a popular social pastime for both participants and onlookers. Given the gulf that had therefore developed between the perception of dance as a secular social activity and the formal, cerebral character of most corporate worship, it is not surprising that the idea of dance as a means of expressing worship was one that would have found little support.

An important transition came with the development of modern dance. As both dance and worship acquired a new freedom of creativity and expression, the gulf between dance and worship diminished. In the same way that there was a blossoming of creativity in church music in the nineteen-sixties, and then drama in the nineteen-seventies, so the eighties have been the years that have seen the more widespread acceptance of dance.

3. SHOULD WE DANCE?
The theological justification of liturgical dance

This consideration of the history of the Christian attitude to dance shows that that attitude has been strongly influenced by the social factors of the culture surrounding the church in two ways. Firstly, there have been times when Christians have wished to distance themselves from cultures which have a debased and corrupted conception of dance, producing an attitude which has thrown the baby out with the bath water, rejecting dance rather than seeking to reclaim and redeem it. Secondly, the prevailing philosophies unconsciously accepted by Western society have made their contribution to the neglect of non-verbal means of expressing worship.

Just as the neglect and condemnation of dance in worship appears to have been culturally rather than theologically determined, there could be a danger that the current revival of interest in liturgical dance is simply a response to our present culture. The ideals of the Enlightenment can be seen to be losing ground in a number of ways; a growing mistrust of science and technology, a resurgence of interest in psychic and spiritual phenomena, an increasingly audio-visual and correspondingly less literate population. There is an emphasis on physical health and fitness that particularly relates to the use of physical movement in worship. This is why it is necessary to give consideration to whether we *should* dance our worship, and not take the idea on board without theological reflection. If it has been unwise to neglect dance because that has been the mood of the philosophy of the age, then it would be equally unwise to introduce it on a similar basis. If, on the other hand, the conclusion is that dance is an acceptable expression of Christian worship, then a clear understanding of the theology of worship involved will enable the justification of dance to those unconvinced, and will provide a basis for being able to discriminate between dance which is genuinely an appropriate offering of worship and that which is not.

There is considerable divergence between the Biblical view of humanity and the Platonic dualism that came to dominate Western thought, despite the Hellenistic influence on Jewish thought in the inter-testamental period. It was the Greek philosophers that identified the person with the soul. To them the body was a prison, in which the soul was trapped; at death the soul was released from the bonds of mortality. Hebrew thought was quite different, seeing the person as an entity. That entity is encountered in both physical and spiritual aspects, but the essential person is not to be identified with one aspect alone, or even with the sum of the parts. The person is not a spiritual being that happens to inhabit a body. It is not consistent with Hebrew thought to speak of the body as a possession, as if the self were something that existed apart from the body.

While Hebrew has words for flesh (*basar*) and soul (*nephesh*), there is a certain interchangeability in the way they are used, particularly in the parallelism of Hebrew poetry. So in Psalm 84:

> 'My soul yearns, even faints
>> for the courts of the Lord;
> my heart and flesh cry out
>> for the living God.'

13

The terms 'flesh' and 'soul' are seen to be ways of describing the totality of the person, rather than suggesting that there are these components that make up a person.

It follows that this Biblical view of the nature of humanity is incompatible with any form of dualism that separates body and soul, particularly when that dualism sees matter as essentially evil. The Bible asserts that 'God created man in his own image; male and female he created them.'[1] That creation includes our physical bodies as integral to our humanity, and as part of the creation that is essentially good. This is supremely seen in Jesus, the Word made flesh, who was fully human yet without sin.

If we are to offer the whole of our humanity to God in worship, that will include the offering of our physical bodies, because to deny that is to deny an inescapable aspect of our humanity, making our offering less than total. The total offering of ourselves, according to this unified view of human nature, is what Paul refers to in Romans 12.1:

'Therefore, I urge you, brothers, in view of God's mercy, to offer your bodies as living sacrifices, holy and pleasing to God—which is your spiritual worship.'

This verse is often used as a proof text by those wishing to promote dance in worship, as if it referred only to the physical. For example, Paula Douthett of The Sacred Dance Group comments on this verse:

'As God's dancers, we are called to present our bodies in worship to him in his presence, using movement as our language of prayer and adoration.'[2]

The 'offering' of Romans 12.1 includes our physical bodies, but to limit its meaning to this is to miss the integration of all aspects of humanity in Paul's thought, and to assume a dualism which is not there. The intrinsic weakness of this exegesis becomes apparent when the same approach is also applied to other passages in which 'the flesh' is denigrated, giving conclusions that are contradictory.

It is also all too easy to read the Pauline passages concerning 'the flesh' as though Paul identifies the physical as the intrinsically evil part of human nature, because of his contrasts between the things of the spirit (*pneumatikos*) and the things of the flesh (*sarkikos*), as, for example, in Galatians 5; particularly as his first example of the works of the flesh in that passage is sexual immorality. Paul does not intend to disparage the physical side of human nature as such. His distinction is between humanity redeemed by God and submitted to him, and humanity in rebellion against God. More recent versions of the Bible make this clearer, translating *sarkikos* as 'the sinful nature' (NIV) or 'the unspiritual nature' (REV). However, the assumption that Christianity disapproves of the physical still lingers in the minds of many.

[1] Genesis 1.27.
[2] P. Douthett, *Spiritual principles of our life and work. The Ministry of Dance: A Vision of Worship*, (The Sacred Dance Group, 1985), p.1.

Several factors have therefore combined to make Christians distance themselves from an appreciation of the physical aspects of humanity as an integral part of human nature. The prevailing philosophies have been those which dismiss the physical and material as being of less value than the abstract and rational. The interpretation placed on scripture has reinforced this view. The 'sinful nature' has been too readily identified with sexual sin.

All of these factors are confronted by the introduction of liturgical dance, and those who wish to encourage dance in worship will need to be sensitive to the reasons why people may find it difficult. Particular care is needed when the problems are related to sexuality. The example of Salome serves as a reminder that dance can be misused to deliberately arouse lust, and there are those who have misgivings that watching liturgical dance, even dance performed from excellent motives, may arouse sexual feelings. Because of the church's preoccupation with sexual sin, it is assumed that such feelings are wrong and should be suppressed.

The difficulty lies in redressing the balance in the attitude of the church to human sexuality. On the one hand, a return to the Biblical understanding of the inter-relation of all aspects of our God-given humanity will encourage us in a proper appreciation of our sexuality, away from the church's obsession with sexual sin. On the other hand, we live in a society whose sexual ethics are so far from God's ideals that we need constantly to check that we are not absorbing and accepting the standards of the world. The path between prohibition and licence may in places seem very narrow. Those who encourage dance in worship need to tread with care, and with pastoral sensitivity.

Another problem over the right use of dance in worship may emerge with those who have swung away from the traditional dualism of Western thought towards a philosophy that goes beyond giving human nature its true God-given worth, and fails to take into account the reality of human sinfulness. This philosophy tends to glorify humanity rather than the transcendent God, who is reduced to the summation of our good. There is evidence of this trend in the present concern with physical well-being. Dance in worship can all too easily become the exclusive province of the young, the fit, and the beautiful. If we dance, it must be to the glory of God. It would be a misuse of a rediscovered gift if a new emphasis on the physical led to an imbalance in the opposite direction and led to the neglect of the other aspects of our humanity and to a distorted theology.

4. CAN WE DANCE?

The introduction and development of dance in worship

(a) The evaluation of current practice

From the consideration of the theological issues that underlie the use of movement and dance in worship, it follows that this is an issue which no church can afford to ignore, whether or not it has an identifiable dance ministry. It has been stressed that all corporate worship involves movement, and that movement inevitably conveys a message. In a society in which communication is increasingly visual, the message conveyed by the visual impact of the liturgy is more significant than it was in generations in which reading and hearing predominated. Rather than deploring this trend, a church can use it as an opportunity to review the movement and dance used in its worship; to acknowledge the integrated character of human nature that is the Biblical doctrine of humanity; and to examine whether or not that is given expression in worship.

The evaluation of movement in worship therefore needs to be on the agenda of all congregations who are concerned about their worship, from those who have never given much thought to the possibilities of danced worship, to those where it has become established. The results of such an evaluation might be surprising ... the small village church with fixed pews and traditional services might have its liturgy well choreographed because of the constraints of working in a confined space, so that the movement is simple, unfussy, and directs the attention of the congregation appropriately ... the church that has reordered to create space for dance and drama might habitually clutter the same space with trailing microphone leads and the cases for musical instruments ... the well prepared and executed dances of the dance group may be regarded as a cabaret act by a congregation that feels like an audience...

It follows that such an evaluation can most profitably be carried out by a cross-section of the congregation, and not just by the leaders. It is only by discussion that the leaders will discover what is appreciated and what is merely tolerated; what people would love to join in with and what they would gladly abolish. This consideration of the movement that is already part of the life of a particular worshipping community will enable those responsible for leading worship to appreciate how that community understands movement in worship. That can then be the first step to finding the appropriate ways to develop the worship in dance and movement. If this is done, there is less chance of initiating something that disrupts rather than develops worship.

(b) Moving on

As well as evaluating the specific question of movement and dance in the worship of a congregation, it is helpful to give some thought to a more general consideration of the overall character of the congregation and its worship. The ministry of dance must be a *ministry*; it must find its reason for existence in the service of the people of God, in enabling them to express their worship, so that they in turn are built up and strengthened in their faith and enabled to serve Christ as they are called.

This consideration of the primary need to serve the congregation as is best for them might mean that those who have first caught the vision of the possibilities of danced worship may have to exercise patience and restraint. There are too many people around who shudder at the memory of their first encounters with liturgical dance and who are wary of trying again. The patience may be needed to wait for the appropriate moment; for instance, a church that has recently changed its pattern or style of worship may have had as much innovation as it can handle for a while. The need may be for teaching, from the pulpit or in housegroups, to challenge people to examine their conception of the purpose of worship, or to address the issues discussed in the previous chapters. Those who have the vision need the willingness to keep bringing it before God in prayer, to ensure that it is his vision and not just their enthusiasm; they need the humility to accept the frustration of waiting for others; and they need the wisdom and discernment to introduce the right ideas at the right time.

Given that the time is opportune, dance can be introduced into the worship of a congregation either by introducing more congregational participation in movement and dance in worship, or by starting a dance group. Of these the second approach has probably been the more common; the idea of one enthusiast finding a few volunteers who will then produce such wonderful liturgical dance that everyone else will be won over is very attractive, and far less daunting for the clergy than the prospect of introducing even simple dance or movement to the whole congregation. However, this congregational approach has much to commend it, and is widely used by The Sacred Dance Group.[1]

To appreciate that the results obtained by these two methods are likely to be different, an analogy can be drawn with church music. Music in worship operates in three ways. Firstly, there is congregational singing in which everyone participates. Being tone-deaf, or not really knowing the tune, or not being able to reach the high notes, is no bar to joining in. Of course, an experienced worship leader chooses material that is within the capabilities of the congregation, otherwise the embarrassment of the poor standard of the overall effect hinders people in using the music as a means to express their worship, but provided the material is chosen with care in this way, all those present should feel able to participate.

Secondly, there is the church choir or music group. Those who belong to this group are those with musical skills which they offer in the ministry of the church's music. The group will provide a lead for the congregational singing, and will give time to the preparation and rehearsal of music to be used in worship. They may also make their own contribution to the worship, when they will sing and the rest of the congregation will listen.

Thirdly, there is the professional cathedral choir, of whom a higher standard of rehearsal and performance is demanded. The congregation at a cathedral service does not generally expect to join in with much of the music at all!

[1] P. Douthett, *Spiritual Principles of our life and work. How to Lead People into Praise and Worship. Part I: Through Congregational Participation*, (The Sacred Dance Group, 1986).

The same three types can be found in liturgical dance; congregational participation for everyone, the dance group, and the professionals. As with the music, all three levels can be a means of worship, even though the amount of participation decreases as the standard becomes more professional. There is then an increasing temptation to be a spectator rather than becoming involved in the worship in heart and mind, even if not with feet or voice. The ability to resist becoming a mere spectator, not entering into the worship, is partly dependent on the memory of participation at the congregational level. That is why the congregational approach makes a good introductory route for liturgical dance. The progress may seem to be slower than introducing a dance group, but the congregation will have experienced the participation in danced worship for themselves, and will have made it their own. They will gradually be ready to move on to involvement in worship watching a dance group with far less danger of feeling relegated to the role of spectator.

(c) Introducing congregational movement
The decision about the type of movement to be introduced in a particular congregation will depend on the conclusions reached about the movement already incorporated in the liturgy. It will often be possible to build on that which is already used, by widening the participation in movements formerly restricted to those with particular functions in the liturgy. Other changes may need to be more innovative.

Whatever is done, the introduction will benefit from explanation. There will be far greater willingness to co-operate if people understand the significance of what is suggested and are therefore able to engage in the movement as part of their worship. It is a mistake to expect people simply to copy movements. If the explanations are made, and then an invitation to join in is given, those present can make their own decision as to whether or not they participate without being pressurised. There are a number of categories of movement which have been found to be helpful, and it is worthwhile for those responsible for worship in a congregation to consider the extent to which these are already being used, and whether there are others that would enrich the worship.

Movement prayers: congregations can be encouraged to find appropriate movements to express the meaning of familiar prayers. Where a prayer is corporate, the highly individualistic 'heads bowed, hands together, eyes shut' position familiar from school assemblies can completely contradict the words spoken. The words of the Grace '. . .and the fellowship of the Holy Spirit be with us all . . .' make more sense with eyes open, looking at one another, and perhaps holding hands with one another. The Lord's Prayer lends itself to movement using simple gestures to embody the sense of each phrase; this is particularly effective when sung, as the music provides a rhythmical framework, and might well be appropriate in the action of the Eucharistic liturgy. It is extremely valuable to give the opportunity for congregations to develop their own movements. Those from different age groups and different cultures will bring differing movement vocabularies to their worship, as they draw on a variety of dance traditions.

Movement songs: these are only a small step from movement prayers. It is a good idea to use songs in which the words express the offering of worship, which can be reflected in the movements made. These are more likely to engage with the experience of 'wonder, love and praise' that is worship than the actions of the 'wise man built his house upon a rock' variety. The Psalms have a movement vocabulary built into them; this can be used in conjunction with their musical settings to give physical expression to the emotions of worship. Songs such as those from the Vineyard Fellowships might also find a place here, not least because their repetitive style frees people from their dependence on hymnbooks. Someone able to use sign language could help with the development of a movement language for worship. This would have a particular significance in a congregation which included people who were profoundly deaf, but there would be much that any congregation might value.

Processions: these can be very enjoyable provided the space is adequate, and they do not have to be restricted to the clergy and choirs. There are good ideas in *The Promise of His Glory,* as well as adequate space, the other main ingredient to bring the ideas to life is imagination (and candles!). Other festivals in the Church's year will provide their own inspiration.

Celebrations: many churches have a Harvest Supper, or similar social occasions, which may include barn dancing as part of the celebrations, even in churches which would normally be very wary of danced worship. This provides an opportunity to challenge the division of life into secular and sacred from the opposite perspective. If the occasion is Harvest, the celebration and dance is surely as much a part of the offering of thanksgiving to God as is singing the harvest hymns. Useful links can be made with the Jewish festivals, and the psalms. Israeli circle dancing, familiar to many from visits to Lee Abbey, is thoroughly enjoyable and an excellent ice-breaker for getting reluctant dancers involved, but is also a means of making the connection between dance and worship.

These are a few suggestions that might enable the beginnings of liturgical dance in a church, or broaden the scope of what is being done. It is good if ideas for a church are generated within that congregation. When considering ideas from other sources, it is not safe to assume that what works in church A will also work in church B. Dance and movement depend on space, and this will vary with the individual buildings and their architecture and furnishings. For example, a procession that involves the entire congregation moving from the font to the sanctuary would be feasible in a church with a congregation barely into double figures, in a way that would be utterly impossible in a church that was packed to the doors. The movement that is possible during prayers will depend on whether the custom is to kneel or to sit, and on the type of chairs or pews. The dynamics of movement in a church arranged in the round are different from those in a church with a traditional nave and chancel.

Increased congregational participation may well produce frustration with the limitations imposed by the architecture. There is much to be said for working within the limitations until they are recognised to be unbearable rather than rushing into change at the first opportunity. Church of England churches are in any case bound by Canon F13 to obtain a faculty or licence for such changes.

It is important that those who are enthusiastic about congregational involvement in movement in worship should be sensitive to the reluctance of others. This is where the understanding of the theological issues involved is important. For some, particularly those whose spirituality has been nurtured in more traditional ways, the reluctance will stem from a deep sense that dance is not what one is supposed to do in church. With gentleness and patience, it is possible to widen their vision of worship, without devaluing that which they have.

There will also be times for everyone when they will find that being involved in movement and dance in worship is threatening. We are learning to be more aware of the power of non-verbal communication; our bodies reveal our true thoughts and feelings even when our words disguise them. We may well be able to sing and say words of adoration or repentance or forgiveness, when our inward attitude is anything but that, but if we are asked to express such attitudes in movement we will be acutely aware of the contradictions within ourselves. Movement and dance may therefore unearth pastoral needs that had been hidden. Equally, objections to involvement in movement and dance may indicate a reluctance to acknowledge such need.

From the beginnings of congregational participation in movement, a church can develop its worship, either with more elaborate movement and dance for the congregation as a whole, or by establishing a dance group. If the congregational participation becomes more elaborate, care is needed to ensure that individual members of the congregation are not excluded or embarrassed by the complexity, the same danger that was noted in the analogy with congregational music. Those in danger of being excluded in this way include those who are very young, elderly or infirm, and those with disabilities. Also, most congregations are likely to include new members, either new to Christian faith or new to the area; these too may feel excluded. If this is happening, it would probably be wise to keep the congregational movement at a level everyone can cope with, and develop a dance group for those who wish to explore the ministry of dance further.

5. CAN THEY DANCE?

The Dance Group

This is the point at which this booklet might have been expected to start, rather than it being relegated to the last chapter. However, the reason for covering the earlier ground is to provide a basis on which the ministry of the dance group can then be built. The worship leader who has thought through the theological and historical issues discussed in earlier chapters will be in a better position to assess the contribution made by a dance group to the worship; the congregation that has begun to understand the role of dance in worship through having the opportunity to participate in dance and movement, will be much better equipped to receive from the ministry of a dance group than one that has not.

As mentioned earlier, most of the available literature on dance in worship is practically orientated and is addressed to those involved in a dance group or similar situation. This booklet has neither the space nor the intention to duplicate such material, but will provide some indications of the role a dance group plays within the worshipping life of a church, and how a dance group can co-ordinate its work with those responsible for other aspects of worship.

(a) Leadership
If a dance group is to be an established part of a church, then it will need leadership. This will not generally be provided by the clergy; even if they have the necessary competence they are unlikely to have the time. Even if they have, the importance of lay ministry is being increasingly recognized within our churches. If it is appropriate for a particular church to have a dance group, it would seem strange if the only people capable of leading it were the clergy. It is not unusual for the emergence of a person suitable to lead a dance group to be a determining factor in initiating dance in a congregation. Such a person can be used to lead congregational movement, and to run workshops.

The role of a dance leader is best viewed in the same light as that of organist and choirmaster. They are the people with the necessary competence in their particular art. They act as a professional resource for others in the group, supplying ideas and material. They are the people who are able to train and encourage others, who can teach new skills and draw out the creativity of the group.

As well as such professional competence, those involved in leading worship need the spiritual maturity to be able to submit their gifts to the service of God and to be able to work co-operatively with others responsible for worship. Too many churches suffer from poor relationships between the clergy and the musicians, and it would be tragic to compound this with dance leaders. Canon B20 makes it clear that the minister has overall responsibility for worship with regard to music. Dance leaders would be well advised to work under the same provision, acknowledging that the responsibility for worship is a part of the minister's pastoral charge.

Dance leaders will therefore need to be able to liaise with clergy, who in turn will need to understand the needs of the dancers. An effective piece of danced worship may take several weeks of preparation; the second week in December is not adequate notice for 'something for the Carol service, please'.

Co-operation between dancers and musicians needs careful thought. Using taped music has the advantage of total consistency for the dancers, but raises issues of copyright and adequate PA systems, and may make the musicians in the congregation feel devalued. A good leader will have the pastoral sensitivity to anticipate such situations and to handle them wisely.

There is a good case for the leadership of a dance group to be exercised jointly, for several reasons. It has been noted that the use of dance in worship is likely to unearth pastoral needs, and this is particularly true for those in a dance group, who are making a greater commitment of themselves to dance than the general congregation. It has been noted that those needs may well touch on issues related to sexuality. It may therefore been seen as prudent to have both men and women in the leadership team. It is also likely that the majority of those who would wish to belong to a dance group will be young. It may be thought wise to attach to the group one or two more mature Christians, with proven pastoral gifts, who will be able to help those less experienced and provide an assessment of the dance prepared.

There is an important place in the leadership team for the apprentice. If a dance group is heavily dependent on the leadership of one person, it is apt to flounder if that person leaves. It is not easy to leave a new dance leader starting from scratch a record of what has gone before. An apprentice leader will learn the skills of leadership as well as the traditions of the group, equipping them to continue the work as need arises.

(b) Workshops
As the use of movement and dance is established in a congregation it will become apparent that there are those who have particular gifts in this area, who should be encouraged to offer their gifts in a dance group. One way towards this can be through organizing dance workshops. If dance is introduced to a church by means of a dance group rather than through congregational participation, a workshop to find potential members would often be the first step.

Through the workshop format, those who wish to can pursue the possibilities of dance in worship further. It is important at the stage of inviting those interested to participate in workshops to stress that that means *participate*. Because dance is such a personal form of expression and one in which many are not fully at home with themselves, the added embarrassment of having an audience of those who 'don't want to join in, but would like to come and watch' will be detrimental to the success of the workshop.

After a workshop, there will often be pressure for the results to be seen. This may come from those who have taken part who want to share what they have learnt, or from clergy who are keen to introduce dance (after all, that's why they organised the workshop . . .) Careful consideration should be given to going public in this way. The time for rehearsal will have been short, and those dancing have not had time to get used to working together. A poor performance will do little to reassure the reluctant.

(c) Belonging to a dance group
The next move from dance workshops, which are usually 'one-off' or occasional events, is a dance group which is a regular commitment for its members. It is vital to stress to those wishing to be part of such a group that the primary purpose of the group is to serve the worshipping community through the ministry of dance. Again, the analogy with music is helpful. Those who wish to be part of the church's music solely as an opportunity to sing would be better advised to join the local choral society. Those who wish to dance must feel called to use that gift in the service of the Lord in the worship offered by his people. The church may wish to emphasise this by publicly commissioning the dance team and thus providing them with the chance to dedicate their work to God.

Belonging to a dance group requires commitment from its members. They must be prepared to train and to practise individually, and corporately. Even more significantly, they must be willing to be committed to the other members of the group within the Body of Christ. The dance of the group will grow out of the worshipping life of the group. Time spent together in prayer, Bible study and fellowship is of greater importance than rehearsal time. The mutual trust and deepened relationships that are built up in this way will be communicated in the dance and give a reality to the gospel of grace that is proclaimed in worship.